Your Money Matters
A guide to your financial life

Greg Saladino

YMMBOOK . COM

This publication is designed to provide competent and reliable information regarding the subject matter covered. However, it is sold with the understanding that the author and publisher are not engaged in rendering legal, financial, or other professional advice. Laws and practices often vary from state to state and if legal, financial, or other expert assistance is required, their services of a professional should be sought. The author and publisher specifically disclaim any liability that is incurred from the application or use of the contents in this book.

GS Books
8927 Hypoluxo Rd, Suite A145
Lake Worth, FL 33467

Printed in the United States of America

Library of Congress in Cataloging in Publication Data

Saladino, Greg
Your Money Matters

ISBN: 9780692046036
LCCN: 2018900023

Contents

About the Author

Intro   1

1.   Calculations to succeed   6

2.   Budgeting   15

3.   Contracts   25

4.   Credit scores   30

5.   Credit cards   40

6.   Purchasing a home   51

7.   Purchasing a car   60

8.   Retirement savings   71

9.   Loans   79

10.   Insurances   84

11.   Debt management   100

Contents

12. Wealth building   104

13. Putting it all together   111
     to manage your life

BONUS CHAPTER   115

For more go to: **YMMBook.com**

About the Author

I was born in Queens, New York and grew up between there and Florida. I was exposed early in life to business and personal finance by my family who always taught me the possibilities are endless. I am thankful every day for that lesson.

An Entrepreneur since the beginning; I started my first business in 5th grade distributing candy. Later while in college started my first organized business selling beepers on campus. This developed into a full service beeper and cell phone store within a few months. I was able to build and sell the store to move into the corporate world working with a Fortune 500 company. I remain with the same company, moving through the ranks to multi-location management in South Florida.

While building my career and wealth I learned that I had a better grasp of personal finance than many of my peers.

Over the years I have given many people advice, friends and peers, developing budgets and helping them negotiate all different financial matters. This led me to begin writing to share my knowledge on personal finance with the world. It began with just a few notes and evolved into the idea of writing this book.

My goal and mission of this book is to bring the knowledge of personal finance to as many people as possible and to make every generation savvier in matters of personal finance.

Acknowledgements

I want to thank my family for supporting me in this project.

You sacrificed with me every step of the way.

Thank you for putting up with my 60-70 hour work week and still pushing me to keep going on this book in my down time.

This book could not have happened without you!

Intro

Thank you for purchasing Your Money Matters. This book will help you manage your financial life so you never fall victim to not knowing or understanding finance.

In this book I will not teach you to be a financial genius, but I will give you strategies so that you can manage your day to day life. This will teach you to navigate through finances without being stressed every time a financial situation arises.

When you are in school, you are taught to continue your education and when you are done you will be awarded a good job. During this time no matter how far you go in school, you will not learn about personal finance. Without this knowledge, you will spend the next 40-50 years trying to accumulate enough money to not have to work, or "retire".

This book will teach you what school left out. It will show you how to manage your money so you don't work your whole life just to survive!

Our world has been through recent financial crisis due to people not being taught how to manage their money. It was not the banks that signed loans that they didn't understand, they were in business to make money on interest and their risk in many cases did not work out. While it can be debated whether or not the banks or the individuals were at fault, if the people knew about finance it would not have been such a major issue. Most of this crisis was caused by people not knowing how to manage their financial life.

The lucky people whose parents took the time and had the knowledge to teach them are able to do well and prosper no matter what the government is doing with our tax dollars. Yes, I know, the government is in the same boat, but that doesn't give you an excuse to work till your 70 and have nothing to show for it.

We will teach you in simple terms how to manage the money you make to maximize your potential. It doesn't matter if you are in high school, just starting college or you have been in the work force for several years. The main goal I had when I started writing this book is to teach as many people as possible how to manage their money.

The more I talked to my friends and colleagues the more I realized; most people do not have a clue on how to manage their finances.

I knew going into this that a book on finance needs to be simple and concise so people can refer to it with ease. My desire was to make it interesting to capture my audience's attention so they can learn this very valuable lesson.

Personal finance and the disciplines that come with it are not fun and are a challenge to make interesting. There are many things in this book that you will probably not be willing to do. You might have to change some of your beliefs and erase some of the poor money habits that you learned.

We are going to cover a lot of things from credit cards to saving and when you read this book you will have the basic knowledge to Navigate through any financial times. Whether you make $15,000 a year or $350,000 a year this book will help you learn the basic financial things that everyone should know.

That being said, my book is broken into chapters that you can use as needed as each chapter is not cumulative. Each chapter stands on its own and tells you exactly what you need to know about the given subject. An example of this would be in the "purchasing a car" chapter.

If you are going to purchase a car, you can turn to the section and get all the info you need to purchase the car, from negotiating the deal to making the loan that is right for you situation. The chapter will tell you what you need without reading the entire book. I have found that this is the most useful way to use this type of book. The book will give you the tools that anyone can use to learn how to navigate through the challenges that you will face.

Debt equals stress. Some people say that some debt is good; I will tell you that no debt is good. Debt and financial issues cause more divorces than any other issue. The stress that comes from being in debt is overwhelming.

There is a way out if you learn to manage your finances. If you follow the lessons of this book and you are just starting out you will never allow yourself to get into debt in the first place. If you are already in a situation this book will help you focus and recover from it and start building your financial future.

Thank you for purchasing my book and I hope that it helps you manage your financial life. You have made a small investment purchasing this book and started the process of realizing that **YOUR MONEY MATTERS!** Good luck as the master of your financial future. By reading this book you will have the tools to effectively master your financial universe.

Chapter 1

Calculations to succeed

As I said in the introduction of the book, I want to teach as many people as possible to grab a hold of your financial life now. Before you can become an expert at running your financial life you need to make sure you understand simple calculations.

I have learned throughout the years that some people are quick to learn these calculations and some are not. We are taught some of this while in grade school, but it is not related to life. When we go out into the world a good majority of people do not know how loans or interest is calculated. I have broken this down into 4 main things you need to know.

These calculations are something I thought of as common knowledge, but it turns out a lot of people do not know how to use them.

We will go over all four of these and we will go over each in as much detail as possible without making this too complicated. I highly recommend reading this and making sure you completely understand all these calculations before moving on to the other chapters. These calculations relate to any transaction you will do in your financial life.

1. Averaging
2. Simple and compound interest
3. Calculating Percentages: How to calculate how much an item will cost if you finance it.
4. How to fit it into your budget.

Averaging:

Averaging is used for almost everything we do in this book. All planning involves averaging and without this simple rule you cannot plan any of your goals.

So how is averaging going to help me be debt free and end up not having to work for the rest of my life? Let's start with some examples of how you use averaging.

The first thing is rather elementary, but I feel it is necessary to discuss and that is to define Averaging for this book. Averaging for our purpose is planning based on history.

We base our averages on history so a good example of this is trying to average what you spend in a given month.

Example: Mary is gathering information to form a budget. She sees that her spending pattern was the following.

June, July and August you spent $1200, $1500, and $1300 your average spending per month is $1333.

In this example the calculation is:
$1200+$1500+$1300= $4000.
Then divide $4000 by 3, which gives you the average of $1333.

She now has a base amount that she spends on average each month. Her average monthly spending is $1333.

Here are some further examples on how we can use averaging in some of our savings and budgeting.

1. Credit card minimum payments.
2. Payments on an acquired item.
3. The amount you can forecast to make in the future.
4. The amount you can save in the next year.

There are some more calculations that you need to be familiar with which leads us to the next "fun" topic of discussion, Interest!

Interest:

Interest is the extra money you pay to borrow money.

This is one of the biggest things that stop people from generating wealth. When you go to a bank and borrow money they will set up a loan for you and tell you how much you will pay every month. The payment includes the banks fee for loaning you this money which is called interest. This fee varies based on credit worthiness and the type of bank you are borrowing from, but normally ranges from 2%-27%.

The calculated interest rate makes a big difference in the payment and total amount you will pay for borrowing the money. These interest rates are based on your credit worthiness. You can save big or spend big based on your credit score. We get more into this in the Credit Score section and we discuss how you can make sure you have the lowest rate possible.

Getting back to the task at hand, there are two main types of interest you could end up paying in your financial life, Simple and Compound interest.

Simple interest:

This is the easiest type to calculate and also the one that ends up costing you the least amount of money. Simple interest is defined as interest based only on the principal. As an example, if you borrow 1000 at 5% interest for 1 year you would owe $1050.00 at the end of the year.

As you pay down the balance you pay less interest and more principal until the loan is paid off. You can use the following formula to calculate this type of interest on anything you borrow.

Formula:

SI [Interest] = (P × R × T) / 100
S [sum] = (SI × 100) / (R × T)
R [Rate/year] = (SI × 100) / (P × T)
T [Time] = (SI × 100) / (P × R)

Key
S.I. = Simple Interest
S = Principle or Sum of amount
R = % Rate per year
T = Time Span

Compound interest:

Compound interest is the type you pay on credit cards and other revolving types of credit. This interest is a very costly way to borrow money. To make it simple for this book, you keep paying more as the interest accumulates.

Example:

The first day of a $1,000 loan you would owe $1,000.13. Now the interest is based off the new higher amount. At the end of the day you will end up paying $1051.27. This is the type of interest that credit cards use to keep you in the loop. Looking at this further in the course of 30 days, the interest would go something like this at 5%

Formula:

The formula for annual compound interest, including principal sum, is:

$$A = P(1 + r/n)^{(nt)}$$

Key
A = the future value of the investment/loan, including interest
P = the principal amount (the initial deposit or loan amount)
r = the annual interest rate (decimal)
n = the number of times that interest is compounded per year
t = the number of years the money is borrowed for

As you can see you end up paying more on a compound interest loan then on a simple interest loan. This is very powerful for not only what you owe, but how you will make money. This also works for your savings and investments.

Calculating Percentages:

As you can see compound interest can work to your advantage (with investments) or disadvantage (with debt). You're reading this book to learn and to make sure you use it to your advantage to build wealth.

Credit card loans use compound interest and that is the reason they can be very dangerous as far as your financial future.

This is why credit card companies are now forced to show, on your statement, how much you will be paying if you only pay minimum payments or a certain amount every month.

This same compound interest works to your advantage when you are saving money, say in a 401k program. The money grows, as you save, you make interest on top of the interest you have already earned. Knowing how interest works is very important, in planning.

In some cases, it is worth financing something if you are making more interest in your investments to have to pull that money out to buy something.

Calculation Example:

You want to purchase a car and the interest rate is 4%. You have the cash in your investment accounts and you are averaging 13% in your investment account. If the car costs $30,000 and you finance it for 36 months it will cost you approximately $3,200 to finance for that time period. At the same time, if you leave that $30,000 in the investments and you keep making the 14% the next 3 years you will pay for the interest for that loan, plus have an additional $12,400 earned on the investment. In this case, it is financially smart to take a loan for the car and leave the money in investments to earn more money.

There are many other examples that this can work out. The best way to judge is just do the calculation in any situation you are in. Always calculate the best way to utilize your money.

Fitting into your budget:

This is the part that takes discipline. We are going to discuss budgeting in the next chapter, but the simple fact is once you know how much something is going to cost you, you need to make sure you can afford it.

The next chapter will teach you how to budget and fit everything you can manage into your budget.

Chapter 2

Budgeting
Build a foundation with your budget
Just because your parents couldn't doesn't mean you can't.

Why do we need to budget? A budget is simply a balance of money coming in and money going out. This should include at least 10% for savings.

Budgeting is a lost art due to the generation before us not being able to successfully manage their budgets. If your parents did not know how to budget, chances are they never taught you to.

This chapter will teach you to not spend more than you make and the consequence, if you do. I have some examples you can use on how to make a good budget. Many people in the world consistently over spend to the point that they are paying more out than they make. This is not a situation you want to be in. This is a vicious cycle because you are now working to survive.

No matter what point you are at you can fix it. Although some cases take more time than others there is always a strategy that will enable you to get into a better situation. So, therefore, the first rule in budgeting is DON'T BUY THINGS YOU CANT AFFORD!!

Credit cards are the biggest mistake that people make with their budget; they allow you to spend money that you do not have. If you are maxed out on minimum payments, take your cards and cut them up. By continuing to pay and then charge again you are keeping a cycle of debt in your way of being free. We will talk more about credit card debt later in the book.

Let's look at the basics on how we can see exactly where we are now. Here are some steps you can take to get a base to your budget.

Step 1: Figure all income after taxes (if commission based average the last 5 months).

Step 2; Figure all fixed expenses (rent/mort, car payment, insurance, electric, minimum credit card payments, etc.

Step 3: Subtract Fixed expense from income (this is what you have left for food, entertainment, clothing).

Step 4: Estimate variable expenses (if available, average last 3 months).

Step 5: Set savings goal.

Step 6: Subtract variable expenses from step 3 balance.

This will give you the amount you will have left at the end of each month.

Budget Plan example
Figure 1

MONTHLY BUDGET	PLAN
Mort/tax/.	$800.00
HOA	$222.00
Electric	$225.00
Water Bill	$35.00
Cable	$90.00
Phone	$45.00
Cell Phone	$150.00
Car	$354.00
Car Insurance	$102.00
Gas	$140.00
Home insurance	$138.00
Food	$450.00
C.C.	$400.00
Entertainment	$400.00
College tuition	$265.00
Lunch/Dinners	$300.00
Misc.	$200.00
Total	$4316.00

*Over estimate expenses on this section, this should be worse case scenario. If you do this budgeting model and have a positive you are in a good position.

Figure 2

SALARY	Plan	Actual	Variance
Wife	$2,500	$2,500	$0
Husband	$2,200	$2,500	$300
Total	$4,700	$5,000	$300

As you can see by the budgeting model, it's simple. You get all your income and revenue written down and then you go from there.

In the case of Figure 1&2, the married couples used as the example are making $5000.00 after taxes and make more money than they spend. They end up with $684.00 available to save if they stick to the budget. In this case, they make a good living and are able to save over 10% of their net income. This money can be used to save or invest.

If they just save this money and put it in a bank account, in 4 years they will have enough to purchase a nice car in cash money. In 10 years they will have over $82,000, and that is without any interest that they would earn as the money builds.

Say they are sticking to the budget, now is the time to see what you need and what you don't need. The first thing to look at is your fixed expenses. These are as stated above and are generally your mortgage/ rent, car payment, and fixed loans.

These can only be changed if you consolidate loans to pay less in interest and there are many ways to do this. If your credit is good you should not have an issue doing it if your interest rates warrant it.

The next thing you need to look at is your variable expenses; these are electric, food, going out, gas, etc. Everything I list in the spreadsheet that changes from month to month.

This is where you can make an impact on your budget. Cutting down on how much you go out to dinner, cutting down on going out, and reducing clothing/merchandise spending, putting your thermostat up, etc. Making and following a budget is the first step to making yourself free from stress and debt.

The next scenario is quite different:

Budget plan Example

MONTHLY BUDGET	PLAN
Mort/tax	$800.00
HOA	$222.00
Electric	$225.00
Water Bill	$35.00
Cable	$90.00
Phone	$45.00
Cell Phone	$200.00
Car	$690.00
Car Insurance	$140.00
Gas	$250.00
Home insurance	$138.00
Food	$700.00
credit card min	$500.00
Entertainment	$600.00
College loan	$265.00
Lunch/Dinners	$300.00
Misc.	$200.00
Total	$5,400.00

Figure 2

SALARY	Plan	Actual	Variance
Wife	$2,500	$2,500	$0
Husband	$2,200	$2,500	$300
Total	$4,700	$5,000	$300

In this example, the couple, we are reviewing, is spending more than they make and we need to find out where to cut.

We need to look at all controllable expenses starting with leisure and clothes shopping; those are top over spending areas. As you can see we have about $900 in entertainment and lunches/dinners out. That is the first place to start as they are going over what they make by $400 per month. Say we can reduce those two categories to $500 per month. Now we're net even, meaning we are spending exactly what we make.

The next step is to look at all the things we might be able to change. Can we get a better plan for our cell phones? Do we need all the cable channels we currently have? Where can we save now? These are the questions you must ask yourself when you are in a position that you are spending more than you are making. You have to put a stop to it because eventually it will catch up to you.

Once you can get your household at a point where you are breaking even now it's time to have a savings plan. It depends how far you want to take the budgeting, but if you can save $10.00 in each category you have another $100.00 for savings. The whole idea here is to create balance and make sure you do not have to work until you are too old to enjoy retirement.

Now that you have established what your budget should be comes the hard work, sticking to it. If you set an out to eat budget of $30 per week you cannot go spend $60 or you are wasting your time. Make a reasonable budget and stick to it. If you have a family, get everyone involved, including your kids. This will teach them what you are learning. Challenge and reward yourself each month for sticking to the budget.

It will be hard to go from not having a budget to sticking to a strict budget. You will have some pitfalls, I am sure. You will over spend and make some mistakes along the way, but once you are tracking what you do on monthly basis your life will become much easier to manage.

It is up to you to be able to manage your finances. By using the tools in this book to guide you, I am sure, you will be in a better situation then you were before reading the book.

The goal is to save for the time you do not want to work anymore. I'm not saying that everyone has to save 10% of their income to be successful,   but it is a smart goal to have. Using the budgeting tools in this chapter will provide you a foundation for all you're spending and saving habits.

This is like a diet it will never work unless you make it a lifestyle change. A diet never works unless you change things forever and neither will living with a budget.

Chapter 3
Contracts:
Sign away your life on the dotted line

In the world we live in today a handshake and your word will not get you too far. While the definition of a contract is a verbal or written agreement in today's world you need it in writing. Today everything is a contract or in softer terms, an "agreement". Contracts come in all sizes and lengths and are an important tool used in business and consumer purchases, every day.

I thought to include this chapter because of all the complaints I hear on TV about people losing their homes and getting their cars repossessed. If they would have understood the contract terms they most likely would have never gotten into the situation in the first place.

Most of the time people do not read contracts in full and can miss very important terms that are stated in the contact. Many times these terms can cost them money, if they are not followed.

From your credit card to your cell phone you signed some kind of contract/agreement for all of it. The key here is you must understand anything you sign. Most contracts are long and drawn out with a bunch of legal jargon that relates to the rules in the specific state that you are in.

Contracts are created to protect both the company and the consumer. They are the rules and terms that the service or goods that will be provided are governed under.

The most important thing to remember is that contracts are a normal part of our world and you must make an effort to understand them. If you don't you could end up with a bad deal.
As I stated, previously, almost everything we do from watching TV to powering our homes we sign some sort of contract.

When you apply for a credit card for instance, if you don't read the terms (i.e. contract), you can be paying more interest in your charges that you bargained for. Do not be scared of contracts as they are the only way people do business these days. However, you must read them and understand exactly what you are getting into.

Examples of things that are bought and require a contract:

Satellite TV
Credit card
Cellular telephone
Rental agreement
Water service
Electricity

All of these are forms of contracts and you must know the terms. How many of us know when our electric company will charge us a late fee? It's in the contract I can assure you of that. READ THE CONTRACT!

Anytime you buy anything major you will most likely have to sign some terms or agreement. The major idea I want you to get out of this section is that the contract needs to state what you agreed to. If it is not correct, do not sign it!

A contract is generally pretty simple. It spells out who the contract is with, Party A is the purchaser and Party B is the seller. This will usually include the person's name address, and contact info. Party B will also be named in this section.

The next section spells out what is being purchased or agreed to. The next thing in the document will usually be how much you are paying for the goods or service.

The good thing about contracts is that they have to spell out the specifics of payments, late fees, rules and services. So if you buy something that has a contract not only is the company protected, but you're protected. If you agree that the car you just bought will cost you $300 per month and the contract says that, the place you bought the car from cannot charge you $400 next month. They have to go by the agreement.

This is one of the shortest chapters, in this book, but the main point here is contracts are here to protect you and me and the company that wrote them. We must make sure we read all contracts; if we sign it we read it and get a copy. There is no excuse to sign a contract you have not read. If you do that you are looking for trouble. You also should not be surprised if you miss out or do not get what you bargained for.

Chapter 4

Credit scores and you

Like your reputation it takes a lifetime to build and a moment to destroy

Credit is a wonderful thing if you have it and a terrible thing if you don't. I read a comment the other day that said and I'm paraphrasing, "credit it is like your reputation, it takes a lifetime to build and seconds to destroy"! That is a very true statement in the fact that your credit says a lot about you and how organized your life is. More and more companies are checking credit when you go for a job as a sign of responsibility.

I was lucky in that my parents taught me that credit is the key to building wealth. Not in those words, but they always would communicate the fact that when the bill came in it needs to be paid in full. They also cautioned me when I got my first credit card that it is not play money and a $5.00 item can end up costing $50.00 if you only pay the minimum payment.

I have been instilling in my kids the same knowledge and, hopefully, you can pass it to your children to create a generation of responsible people.

The number one reason you want good credit is that it saves you money. Yes, it's true having great credit saves you money, big time! I do not buy anything I cannot afford and am able to pay in cash. Does that mean I do not use my credit? No, I personally take advantage of any 0% or low interest that a company offers.

The only difference is I make sure that I have the money in hand so that when the total is due the item is paid off. This means the original money that I would have spent was able to sit in my investments and make money. So by borrowing the banks money at zero interest I can leave my money in an account or in investments making xx% interest.

That means I made xx% on my money while borrowing the money for the loan, for free.

Understanding credit scores:

Credit scores are a great mystery on the exact breakdown of how they are rated. These scores are called "Fico". This system was devised and breaks down as follows:

1. 35% Payment history
2. 30% Credit Utilization
3. 15% length of credit history
4. 10% Type of credit accounts
5. 10% Recent inquiries

As you can see by the breakdown there are 5 different factors that make up this score. Your payment history being the most weighted part of its makeup.

What they are saying here is that the most important part of what they are looking for is if you pay your bills. The second thing that they are looking for is how much credit you have, how much you use, and how it is related to how much you make. After that they review how long you have had credit as well as what different types of credit you have.

Do you only have credit cards and now you are applying for a house? Or is your credit varied with car loans, student loans, a mortgage and credit cards?

The last thing they are going to look at is inquires. These are logged every time you apply for credit. They basically want to make sure you aren't going to everyone that can supply credit and taking out a line. This is like an early warning system for them since a loan takes a little while to show up on the actual credit report.

These inquires will show up very quickly and warn them of excessive applications for credit.

There are three major scores, Equifax, Experian, and TransUnion and your score will usually be slightly different on all of them. It will most likely be similar, but they are 3 different reporting agencies that a credit card, bank loan, or car loan will check before determining if or how they will loan you money. The score will be between 300 and 850 with the smaller number being bad and the higher number being good.

Different banks have different base criteria. All of them have a tiered system that determines what interest rate you will pay.

There are different websites/apps that can help you with managing your credit further.
One that comes to mind is CreditKarma.com. This is an excellent free service that helps you manage your credit.

Once they get your score they will determine where you fall in there range. Most promotional rates with zero down and the best interest rates are offered when you have a FICO score of 720 or above.

Credit scores are established to verify your worthiness of being loaned money. If your score is good, a bank or credit company will loan you money. If not, they will either loan you the money at a lot higher of a rate or not at all.

If your credit is bad and you need money your only option is to go through pay day loans or other borrowing avenues advertised on TV. I've seen these at as much as 866% total interest paid by the end of the loan.

The best thing to do here is not get into the trouble in the first place. If you are just starting out follow the budgeting model in our budgeting chapter.

Let's look at what you can do to get going in the right direction.

The first thing I want you to do is get a baseline credit score.

These are available for free once a year from the credit bureaus. Using CreditKarma.com or similar you can monitor it as many times as you want.

If your credit is terrible because of past issues it is not too late to rebuild as I will show you in this chapter. Let's talk about starting from scratch first.

New credit:

You're just starting out and want to get maximum credit potential!

You are looking to build credit so how do you do it? Like I said above it takes time to create good credit, but you have to start somewhere. There are 3 easy steps to creating a good credit report.

1. Get a credit card

2. Get a loan
3. Pay on time

   The first thing you need to do is apply for a credit card. This is an easy way to start. Now you are probably thinking, "This guy is telling us to go into debt". No, I'm telling you to get it and use it to build your credit. Do not use it as a source of free money!
   Once you get this card, your mission is to charge $100 in consumables a month. When the bill comes pay off the entire balance. Using this strategy with a credit card will dramatically increase your credit score. Maintain this program, but do not ever spend more than you can pay at the end of the month. I recommend a few cards and you can go on my website to see my recommendations.
   The next step is to finance/lease a car. Even if you want to pay cash you should finance it and pay it off early which will save you the interest. Once the car is paid off you will see your score shoot up. See the buying a car section in Chapter 7 for details on negotiating the best deal possible.
   Finally, you must pay all bills on or before the date they are due.
   No matter what it is, if you are a delinquent payer you will not build your credit you will be marked a late payer and will never achieve a 720 or higher score.

Damaged credit:

If you have a beacon score of less than 600 you are in serious trouble as far as credit goes. As I said previously, you can fix it, but it will take work and time. If your credit score is this low with established credit means that you do not pay on time and states that you are a risk to loan money to.

There are companies available to help with credit consolidation. In most cases, this is a good idea to do. It just depends on how much debt you have and if there's a way out without damaging your credit any more. The first things that you must do are stop spending money and destroy your credit cards.
Don't cancel the account, just cut the credit cards up NOW! This is the biggest error people make. If you do not stop charging you will never get out of debt.
The next step is to figure out who you owe and create a budget to get all debts paid off. This is a very important step to make sure you pay as little interest as possible. The whole theory here is if you pay it off sooner, than it is due, you will pay less interest than you originally signed on to pay.

Example:

Salary per month after tax: $2300

Money owed:

Mortgage: $150,000 left to pay: $1,250. per month,
7.5% interest
Costs you approx. $27.00 per day just in interest

Car: $6,000 left to pay: $207 per month. 10%
interest
Costs you approx. $1.65 per day just in interest

 Credit Card: $10,000 left to pay: $200 per month
min payment 22% interest; Costs you approx.
$6.02 per day just in interest. This will continue to
go up if you pay only the min. payment because it
is compound interest.

Medical: $1,000 left to pay: (this you can pay any
amount every month and they will not hurt your
credit. I recommend $5 per month)
  So what do you attack first?? The first thing in
this example to pay off is the credit card. The
interest rate is horrendous and if you continue to
just pay the minimum you will end up paying
$27,000. It will also take you 15 years to pay it off
at that rate.

In this example, I would recommend paying $300 to the credit card company every month. If you do this, you will pay off the cc in approximately 42 months at a cost of about $12,600.

This only leaves you $643 per month to pay everything else. You must watch every penny to get yourself out of the debt you have created.

This brings us back to creating a budget that we talked about in the Budgeting chapter.

The above example is just to give you an idea of the thought process behind budgeting to get out of debt. This will put you on the path to become very comfortable with your finances.

It will take time and will definitely not be easy to come from being behind to getting ahead, but it is possible with discipline.

To summarize having a better credit score saves you money which builds your wealth. If you can manage to keep a great credit score you will be a lot better off. You will be able to leverage yourself to get things you need without extra fees and charges.

Work on your credit score and it will help you build your financial life.

Chapter 5

Credit Cards:

Help yourself to the plastic currency and if you are not careful pay for life!!

To fully understand how we got to where we are with credit cards, we must talk about some of the history behind the credit cards.

According to many sources credit cards started back in the 1920's, but some have them recorded as far back as the 1890's. This was originally for stores and customers on an exclusive basis. The credit would be extended for that particular person in that particular store that extended the credit.

As time passed, different stores started accepting other stores cards and that is when the third party credit card suppliers came in. These evolved into what we are currently using.

The inventor of the first bank issued credit cards was John Biggins of Flatbush National Bank in Brooklyn, NY. This was called the "charge it" program and was used between merchants and the banks customers. At the time, the bank would bill the customer directly when they used the cards.

In the 1950's they branched out to have national credit cards, the first being Dinners club. This was a charge card only used for restaurants. The company would pay the restaurant and in turn the card holder would pay dinner's club. They did have to pay the entire amount at the end of the period which actually kept people out of debt; if you didn't pay you couldn't use the card.

As things developed banks started issuing cards that could carry a balance and continue to be used. This was a major opportunity for the banks to make a bunch of money off people buying things. Think about it, they are a broker of goods; they take their percentage as interest. Many times, the cost of the interest outweighed the actual cost of the purchased item, while the banks did not have to keep inventory, as the stores did. Using credit cards are great to leverage and track your expenses, but this is not free money. This is a loan for a short period of time, if you extend the time, you paid more.

All this said they were never meant to allow people to live beyond their means.

If you don't have credit yet or you have damaged credit lets discuss some good strategy on building that credit using credit cards.

I was recently asked by my girlfriend's son, "how am I going to get a car if they will not finance me?" I gave him the same advice I use in the previous chapter, I said to him, "Get a credit card!" He looked at me and said "what is that going to do?" I told him your credit and the building of credit all starts with credit cards. Without applying for a credit card you can never build credit.

Let's talk a little bit about credit cards. As I mentioned previously, credit and credit cards are great tools if they are used correctly. The difference in two approaches with credit can severely impact your life for years to come.

The best story I can tell you about this is how the same opportunity went two different ways.

When I got out of High school and started college I started receiving all kinds of credit card offers. My parents advised me to be careful what I do with the credit cards because you have to pay or you will have bad credit. So through all those offers I applied for 2... One was a master card and one was a Discover card. Master card turned me down, but Discover approved me.

My original limit was $500 and I immediately started using the card. This $500 dollar limit kept me in check because I could not get in too much trouble with it. I will say that at 18 $500 might as well been $50,000 because I didn't have a lot of money. I used this card to establish and build my credit. I put gas, food, car stuff, anything I needed, but every month I paid the balance in full. No payments, no interest.

The same thing happened to my girlfriend at the time, but she did not follow the same path. She applied and received a different card with a bigger limit, actually 3 times the limit I had. She proceeded to go out and buy anything she wanted with this card and in fact got 3 more and did the same with them.

She ran up a total of $4,500 dollars in debt within the first year she had credit. She ended up trying to pay the min payments on each one. That $4500 turned into more than $15000 as she continued to struggle to pay the payments. Eventually, she could no longer pay the min payments as we were just 20 years old by this point.

She had gotten into a major trap that you can get in while dealing with credit cards.

Her credit became damaged and could not be repaired for several years. She thankfully had assistance from her parents and after years was able to repair her credit. I advised her, at the time, not to do it but she did not listen. At that point, I was just a kid so who listened to me anyway, but in hindsight years later she did tell me she should have listened to me.

This is a common story for anyone born after 1970. There is a whole generation of people with damaged credit. About 60% of the people I know have damaged or not great credit. Looking at credit websites, only about 5% of people have a FICO score of more than 720.

As I explained in the building credit chapter, your credit stays with you for your whole life. You can damage it very quickly, but it takes a long time to build it back up.

Damaging your credit can ruin your financial life for a very long time.

I recommend as I did to my girlfriends son, getting one credit card. Use this card to keep track of your expenses and make sure you are not putting anything on it that you cannot afford. Putting things on the card that you cannot afford will put you in a situation that will lead to heartache and worse, bad credit.

There are several different types of credit cards you can choose from and I want to teach you some of the benefits of different programs they offer.

The two most used types of cards are
1. Store cards
2. Bank cards
   (MasterCard/Amex/Visa/Discover)

Store cards are the easiest to get and if you have no credit or damaged credit you can probably get one. Some examples of store cards are the following:

Gas station cards
Macy's card
Best buy card
Target card

These are the first card you should try to get. They usually only give $100-$500 dollar limits. You cannot get into too much trouble with these. I recommend using them and building your credit with these types of cards.

Once you are using and paying store cards you will start getting offers for other cards which are bank cards. They offer the most flexibility and you can use them anywhere. These cards have higher limits and they can easily get you into trouble as far as not being able to pay.

There are a few different cards that are worth mentioning. The following is a rundown of them.

No Annual FEE cards:

Cards with no annual fee are the only way to go in my opinion. I currently use one main card which is the AMERICAN EXPRESS BLUE CASH. It is a no fee rewards card. I highly recommend this card as you establish your credit. Cards such as this allow you to use the card with no annual fee and still pay you a percentage back for using their card. A great thing, especially, if you only charge what you can pay off that month.

Rewards cards:

Reward cards are a way the credit card companies convince you to pay with their card. Most rewards cards charge you a yearly fee in return for paying rewards for every dollar you charge. In many cases this can work out as a benefit, but if you are paying more to use it than what you are getting back it is not worth it. You must figure out how much you need to charge to overcome the fee that they charge you. I recommend not paying for the "honor" of using their card.

There are many cards out there that do not charge you and still pay rewards. I recommend looking for a no fee rewards card such as the American Express Blue cash card that I mentioned before. They offer the rewards without having to pay a fee. No fees equal more money in your pocket.

0% interest new purchase/ balance transfer cards:

These cards are good if you have a specific use for it. An example of that would be if you had a specific large purchase and that store doesn't offer any 0% interest payment plans/ cards. You can use these cards for that type of purchase.

I will warn you, however, read the terms of the contract. Most of these cards let you make a balance transfer or charge for one month and then anything else is put in as an interest baring purchase.

I learned this from my own error. I had a charge balance I transferred to a 0% interest on an all balance transferred card. I also used the card for 2 small purchases that same month; I think gas in the car as they said you had to use it at least once for regular purchases, the first month.

When I got the bill I was being charged interest so I called them. They told me I would continue to pay interest until the balance was paid off because all money was credited to the promotional balance first and once that is paid off than I can pay off the other two purchases.

This seemed like a major scam to me, but reading the contract documents I found it was all spelled out. Thankfully, I had the money to pay for the entire purchase, paid the card off, and immediately cancelled it. Now if I was just charging without having the money to pay, I would have been stuck making payments with interest I thought would work out to zero. BUYERS BEWARE. READ THE CONTRACT.

Annual fee cards:

These cards are good for the benefits, but make sure you are going to use what you are paying for. If you are going to pay for a standard American Express Card you have many services included such as reservations, concierge's service, etc. The same services are also available with their blue cash card so the choice is yours to pay or not to pay.

There are so many cards and there is a right card for everyone. My advice is to read the terms of the contract and make sure you apply for one you can take advantage of. Remember credit cards are a great tool, but they can be a nightmare, if you do not watch what you are doing with them.

In summary, start with a standard store card and build your credit. Credit cards are necessary in today's world, but you do not have to get sucked into the game the banks want you to play. You will be very happy if you can build your credit without going into debt and it will save you thousands of dollars when you need to borrow money through your lifetime.

Credit building lessons

1. Get a credit card.
2. Charge only amounts you can pay off.
3. Pay off the card every month.
4. Build slowly and do not go into debt.

Chapter 6

Purchasing a Home
"The American Dream!"

Owning a home is part of the American dream, but for many it turns into a nightmare. Buying a home is a big step for any person or couple in America. The trick is how do you do it without bankrupting yourself?

The fact is that a lot of the trouble people got in a few years ago was due to mortgages they could not afford. There are several things to consider when buying a home and it is not a decision you should go into lightly. There are many advantages in buying a home vs renting and all those need to be weighed before getting into the process. This is a question that many Americans didn't ask themselves before buying a home.

The biggest myth that I have heard since the boom in the early 2000's was real estate always goes up.

That is not true as we saw the last few years. A home is a place to live and should not be considered an investment. Once you add interest and improvements you will most likely always be in the red when it comes to profit on your home. As you can see in the calculation on the next page even at a 5% per year increase in property value, you will most likely never make money on the purchase. There are people that are investors and buy and sell houses for a living, they obviously can make money but again they do this for a living and in most cases you will not make money living in your home.

Example:

$110,000 purchase price
$20,000 down
$90,000 principal loans for 30 years
5% interest rate = $255,000
$3,500 per year for real estate tax= $105,000
Total = $360,000
Home value after 30 years
$110,000 x 30yr @ 5%. Home value in 30 years
$275,000

After paying for 30 years and before you consider home owners insurance and improvements (painting, carpet, appliances, etc.). You are in the hole for $85000.

That being said, it is much better than renting because if you rent an apartment and pay, say $1,100 per month for 360 months you spent $396,000 and have nothing to show for it. So between the two choices you are better off buying.

Now to the budgeting part, the most exciting part of buying anything responsibly. There are a few questions you need to ask yourself right from the beginning.

1. What can you afford?
2. How long do I plan to live there?
3. How many years do you need to pay it off?

These are the 3 main questions you should ask before starting the process. Once you figure the questions above out you will have to find a bank that will finance your purchase. They will also be able to provide you a real estate agent with a pre-qualification letter. This is a letter from the bank that states you have enough credit to finance xxxxxx amount of money.

This is also where you have to use your budget and on line calculators to see what you can afford.

Banks will usually set the letter a little higher then what your max should really be. Remember if you want to live comfortably and not over extend your finances, be careful here.

It is very important that you figure out what you can afford using the budget tools, in this book, before getting your letter. If you over extend yourself, on a house, it can be a major mistake.

Most banks, since the real estate/ economic crisis of 2008 require 5-20% down depending on your credit score. So before you fall in love with a house make sure you have the down payment in cash.

Now the hunt is on for a home that fits your needs. There are a lot of options and things you must look into when looking for a house. If you are starting a family, I recommend buying a house with that in mind with enough rooms and space to fit the growing family.

The reason I recommend this is that depending on the type of loan you get you could spend most of the first 5 years paying mostly interest on your new home. So if you are planning on only spending 3 years in the home, before you outgrow it, you will be wasting money.

Once you find the home of your dreams you have to secure financing. There are many types of loans and I will map out the most common mortgages for you in these next few pages.

Fixed mortgage:

This mortgage can be from 10 to 45 years. Interest rate is fixed for the life of the loan. This is the safest loan you can get. Your loan will be fixed for the full amount of time for loan.

So if its 3.5% today it will be 3.5% 20 years from now. This is a good idea while interest rates are low because you are locking in cheap money. Below is an example of the amortization schedule covering the first 2 years of the mortgage. As you can see on a $200,000 you do not see interest being paid down very quickly.

Here is an Example of 2 years of Amortization on a $200,000 loan.

DATE	PAYMENT	PRINCIPAL	INTEREST	TOTAL INTEREST	BALANCE
Oct. 2015	$1,013.37	$263.37	$750.00	$750.00	$199,736.63
Sept. 2016	$1,013.37	$274.44	$738.93	$8,933.99	$196,773.55
Sept. 2017	$1,013.37	$287.05	$726.32	$17,719.77	$193,398.87

As you can see your total interest in the first 2 years is almost $18,000, while your principal has gone down less than $7,000.

Benefits:

Fixed rate (interest is low now)/ same payment for the whole loan.

The second loan I will discuss in this chapter is the Adjustable rate mortgage. This can be used if you think interest rates will go down. This is most likely a loan you do not want to use but I will go over it anyway. The Adjustable rate loan recalculates itself annually and goes up and down with the market.

Adjustable rate mortgage:

This mortgage can also range from 10-45 years and the interest rate varies for the life of the loan. There is generally a cap on how high the rate can go and is usually based on the 1 year Treasury note or the LIBOR average. This is a perfect loan when interest rates are high and you expect them to go down.

These loans were also used for interest only loans. These loans are still out there, but they are a little different than the product that was offered before the crash. Now if you want an interest only loan you must qualify based on the payment amount after the total payment kicks in. The interest only loan gives an option for new homeowner to have a home loan that for the first 5 years they only pay the interest on. During this time, the payment is, of course, lower because no principal is being paid.

After the initial 5 year period is done the payment recalculates to not only include the interest, but adds the principal amount to the payment. While this was regarded as "toxic" during the crash, they do have their advantages. To really make one of the loans work for you, it has to be with strategy.

I personally used this strategy when I purchased my current home. My strategy was to pay the interest, but also pay the additional principal each month for the first 5 years. What this did for me is allow me to pay more interest than I would have paid if I got a traditional loan. This type of loan can work for you as a strategy to pay your home off quicker than you normally would. In addition, it gives you the flexibility to be able to pay the interest only amount or to pay principal in addition.

The best loans, at this point in time, are the fixed rate loans as interest rates are most likely not going down further.

Is it still part of the "American dream"? I think so! It's not all bad news because you have to live somewhere. If you rented a 3/2 home for the same time period of time you would spend $360,000 and get nothing back at the end.

So if you are going to live on your own it is a good idea to go ahead and buy something as opposed to renting. It cannot be counted on as an appreciating asset, but in the end, at least you have something to recoup some of your living expense.

All that being said you need to make sure you can afford to actually buy the home you are looking for.

As you saw previously, there are additional things you must account for when figuring out your budget. In addition, you will also be committed to pay the loan back to the bank.

Buying a home is serious business and most likely the biggest commitment that you will have in your life. When you sign on the dotted line you will be committing to payments for between 15 and 30 years depending on the loan you choose.
Make sure you know your budget, you choose your product correctly and you have secured the best interest rate possible.

Purchasing a home is a serious decision that you must consider all factors and make sure it fits into your budget.

Lessons for Buying a Home:
1. Figure out your budget
2. Secure financing
3. Find your home
4. Pick the Mortgage terms that fit your budget

Enjoy your New home!

Chapter 7

Purchasing a car

Did you pay more for the same car as the next guy??

For most people purchasing a car is not a fun experience. People, for the most part, do not know how to negotiate or know the tricks that the dealers play. There is a ton of information on the internet on buying cars such as general information, calculators, suggestions on how to negotiate, etc.

In this chapter, I will put it in steps to make sure you are able to put it all together.

5 things that you have to know before you visit the dealer:

1. Which model are you looking for new or used
2. Do you want to buy or lease
3. How much you want to pay
4. How much interest you are willing to pay (establish a budget)
5. How much your trade is worth (this can be found on many sites)

* A good plan, if possible, is to go in the afternoon on the last day of the month. The sales people will be fighting to get more units for higher commission.

The first thing you want to do is compare the cars in the segment (i.e. SUV, luxury, sports, etc.). The internet is a great tool for this. Once you have narrowed it down to a few choices, go drive them. This is necessary and fun because with a car everyone is comfortable with different features and driving characteristics. By driving the cars you should be able to limit your choice to one or two different vehicles.

Once you find out the type and model you want, you have to decide whether you buy new or used. If you buy used you will most likely be purchasing the car to own it as opposed to leasing it.

There are benefits to buying new and benefits to buying used. A car is a depreciating asset that you will never make money on. As soon as you drive a new car off the lot it has lost money. This isn't that big of deal if you are leasing or plan on keeping the car for an extended period of time. You can avoid this dramatic drop in value and as a matter of fact take advantage of it by buying a slightly used car.

Decide whether you want to own or lease your car. This is a simple question that can often get complicated and is often used by sales people to defer you from the actual price and make you think you are saving money. Neither is good or bad and both have advantages and disadvantages.

A good rule of thumb is if you are planning on keeping a car for 6 years or more buy, but if you like a new car every 3-4 years it is a no brainer to lease. A new car is very simple, it is a new and unused vehicle that has a full warranty and has never been registered before.

Used cars break down a little different and here are some used car Basics:

Pre-owned cars are a great alternative to buying a brand new car. There are many pre-owned cars out there and there are different ways to buy. One thing that you should always get is a car fax report to make sure it isn't a salvage or accident car. It is also recommended that you have a mechanic check the car out before purchase.

1. Certified pre-owned:

This is what I call the dealer new used car. This car will have a warranty, usually better than the new car one and it will be pretty much perfect. They get typically a 100 point inspection and if anything is wrong, it is replaced. They do not replace fluids, brakes, etc unless it is needed. Do not think just because it's certified that it is completely ready to go. Normally, these are 1-3 years old and in outstanding condition, but they are the priciest used car option.

2. Used with warranty:

This can be a private or dealer sale and is my favorite option. Usually less than 4 years old with some of the remaining warranty left. The Benefit here is you can get a great deal and then (in most cases, check your brand) you can get the same extended warranty as the certified car.

3. Used without warranty:

This can also be private or dealer and can be quite risky. The car has no warranty, but in some cases you can get an aftermarket warranty put on the car. Most require less than 70000 miles. It is a must you get a vehicle history report and a vehicle inspection by a mechanic before you purchase a used car without warranty. This will most likely be the best deal, but not necessarily the best car.

It all boils down to preference, but I would never recommend that you lease a car for longer than the warranty is in place. I break it down even further with my lease vs buy check list.

Let's start first with the Lease. If the following things fit into your situation it is ideal to lease.

Buy VS Lease:

When leasing a car I look for these as the car buying profile.

- Drive less than 15000 miles per year (most max lease mileage is 15k per year)
- Own a business (you can write off the whole lease payment in many cases- check with your tax person)
- You want a new car every 3 years (40-60 % of the depreciation happens in the first 3 years so, if you buy, you will be upside down.)

Leasing is like buying a portion of the car and paying interest on that amount. It is calculated differently and there is usually a set buy out at the end. One tip I always give anyone is do not put money down on a lease, this is not smart and if the car is totaled or stolen you have lost this money. $0 down leases is the way to go although your payment will be a bit higher depending on the end of lease buy out.

The true cost of the lease is down payment + payments = total cost for the term.

You also want to know that if you decide to keep the car that option also makes sense. To figure that out you use the following calculation.

Total to own the Car:

Down Payment + payments + buyout + tax on buyout = ownership cost.

The only true way to find out how much you are paying is to add it all up!

When buying a car I look at the following.

- Drive more than 15000 miles per year
- You can keep the car 6-10 years
- You do not own a business
- A specialty car that you will keep.

Buying is quite simple and straight forward, but it is only the way to go if you are going to keep the vehicle for a longer period of time. Once you determine which is for you, it's time to research.

Now that you have one or two vehicles in mind do the research and find out the invoice price the dealer pays. This information can be found on TRUECAR.COM which is an excellent resource.

With the invoice price you will know how much they can negotiate. The invoice is not exactly what they pay; they also have holdback and incentives. Depending on how much they need to move the car, which may or may not be, passed down to you.

At this point, your mind should be made up and you should not be swayed by a slick sales person to look at other types of vehicles. This is a trick they can play as this eliminates all the knowledge you have accumulated by researching. Your homework counts here, with the average vehicle costing $26,000 this is very important to living a financially successful life.

When you get to the dealer depending on what brand car you are buying you can potentially be swarmed by sales people. At this point, if you did your research you should know just as much as they do about the car you want.

The sales person will likely try to get information from you. How much do you have in your monthly budget? Do you have a trade in? How much do you want to put down? Do you want to buy or lease?

These are common questions and the answers will be used to set his plan to seem to fit your needs perfectly. You want to be vague with your answers to these questions. Do not talk about trade in. That is a trick to throw that into the negotiation. You must establish how much you are going to pay for the car before any other factors can be discussed. Know what you want to pay and do not just look at the payments, this is a trick to get you to pay more.

What most dealers will do is bring you 3 different payment options depending on the type of car. It is usually 36, 48, and 60 months. Payments will be introduced with xxxx down. The questions you ask now is" how much am I paying for the car?" and "what is the interest % this is based on?" You know the invoice, you know your credit score and you know the current interest % for your credit score.

Once we establish the price, interest rate, down payment, and terms, it is time to make a deal. But wait, do you have a trade in? If you don't skip this section or just read along for fun! If you do have a trade you should already have an estimate from you research on how much it is worth. If you followed the instructions you are in control. The sales person will not want to lose the deal because of the trade in.

How I always put it in this situation is "before we make the deal I think I want to trade my old car in". As I said before, this is a curve ball to the sales person.

Now the deal he thought he had is contingent on a trade. As long as you are reasonable with what you want for the trade he will get you, basically, what you want. By this I mean that if the KBB says it's worth $4,000 as a trade in don't expect to get $4,500. Shoot for $3,200-$3,500, most of the time the first offer on a trade in value of $4,000 will be under $3,000.

I once had dealers first offer on a very old SUV go from $2,700 at the start to $4,300 by the time we made the deal. Remember, in some states, you will also get a sales tax benefit from trading your car vs selling on your own.

The price, the trade, and the interest rate are now established. At this point, most dealers will hand you off to the finance department. Once you get to the finance person you have to confirm all the things you discussed with the sales person have to be in writing.

The finance person will try to sell you on interior protection, underbody protection; extended warranties and other add-ons. He/she will give you this in terms of payments not in terms of total cost.

Example: "the extended warranty" will cost you $29.00 per month for 60 months. In this example, if you pay it up front, it would be $1500.00, but if you pay it in the payment you are paying $1,739.95. The point here is, if you add extras, pay them up front or you will be over paying. Also remember as long as a car is under warranty you can usually extend it, at any time the regular warranty is in effect. Once you have checked the contract and made sure everything you agreed to is correct, you have now purchased a car the correct way.

Depending on how you followed these steps you should have made a great purchase. Enjoy your new car.

Chapter 8

Retirement savings:
One day you will not want to work, will you outlive your money?

One of the things I learned a long time ago is you will never be able to be financially secure if you do not learn how to make your money work for you.

It makes sense that as you work your money needs to be working also. Let me repeat, while you are working, make your money work for you!

So how do I get my money to work for me? When you make investments that yield more money, then your money is working for you.

This is very important, not only in creating and building wealth, but also to ensure you do not have to work until you die. If you do not save and invest when you go to retire you will not be able to afford your retirement. Social security will not be as it is at present day; as a matter of fact it might not be around at all.

That being said you have to do something about it, that's the reason you bought this book!

There are many different ways to accomplish this and we are going to talk about them in this chapter.

401K:

The first one we will break down is the 401k. This is a great program and if you are fortunate enough to work at an organization that has one you need to take advantage of it.

A lot of companies offer a 401k plan for you to invest in. This is a very good way to have your money work for you because some of the companies that set up these plans actually pay you to participate. Yes that's right, your company might pay you to participate in the 401k plan by matching a percentage of what you put in.

Do you have a 401k in the company you work for? Many people do not even realize it; many even participate, but do not take an active role in it as some companies automatically enroll you. The company I work for matches 50% of the first 6% that you invest.

So if I invest 6%, I will actually save 9% each year. Let me give you an example so you completely understand.

Example:

Jim makes $45,000 per year and has a 401k that he invests 5% in.

That means each year he is saving $2,250 on his own. The company at the end of the year will add $1,125 to what he saved. (Calculation: $2,250x .50= $1,125).

In this case before the investments made any money, Jim made 50% on the money he saved.

In simple terms, if your company has a 401k and you do not invest you are refusing money the company is willing to pay you. If you can invest the max amount that your company matches you will maximize the earning potential.

The inverse of that is if you are not investing you are leaving xx% in the hands of your company and not in your pocket. Let's dig deeper and assume you are going to participate and make sure you take advantage of this huge benefit.

Depending how old you are and how much aversion to risk you have, there are many different investment products available for you to choose from.

These funds are from stable companies with little to no risk with minimal yield to high risk with the highest possible yield. There are many in between depending on which institutions your company uses. You can have 20 or so investment choices.

There are also tools available through most programs that will assess your risk tolerance and show you what funds you should pick based on the questions you answer. This will not guarantee you will make a great yield, but it will over the long haul make your money work for you.

There is another benefit to this program. It's a tax loop hole, you're feeling rich already. (**there are no tax loopholes, but this does reduce your tax). By investing your money you actually defer paying taxes on the money you invest.

Example:

Income: $45,000 - 401k investment: $2,250. (5%of income) = taxable income: $42,750.

If your tax bracket is 21% then your tax liability has gone from $9,450 down to $8,978. By investing in the 401k, per the example, you have also paid $472 less in federal taxes. Every dollar that you keep in your pocket and not in the governments is earned money.

So let's add that up. Your company paid you $1,125 and you saved $472 in taxes. Just by saving $2,250 you have made $1597 extra dollars and that's without your investment making any money.

401k = both tax savings and extra savings potential

One last benefit to saving your money in a 401k is that you can borrow money from yourself. Yes, that is correct; you can take a loan on your 401k and pay yourself back over time with interest.

There are rules to this, but it is quite simple and if you have to borrow money you might as well pay yourself back the interest and not the bank. See your plan for details on this.

IRAs:

IRA stands for Individual Retirement Account. Think of it as a savings account that you get big tax breaks on. This makes it an ideal way for most people to put away money for retirement. IRA itself is not an investment – It's just a box to keep you stocks, bonds, mutual funds and other assets.

Unlike 401ks, which are provided by the company you work for, most common types of IRAs are accounts that you open on your own. There are others that can be opened by self-employed individuals and small business owners. There are several different types of IRAs, including Traditional IRAs, Roth IRA, SEP IRAs and Simple IRAs.

Unfortunately, each IRA has eligibility restrictions based on your income or employment status. And all have caps on how much you can contribute each year and penalties, in most cases, for withdrawing money before the designated retirement age.

For this exercise we will only discuss Roth IRA and Traditional IRAs.

Roth IRA:

A Roth IRA is an IRA that is limited to certain individuals. This is a post-tax way to invest for the future. Unlike a 401k the money is taxed before you put it in the account, but any withdrawals you make will not be taxed. There are income limits that can restrict you from investing in a Roth IRA. Please check the updated limits before setting your plan. A good website to go to is http://www.rothira.com/

Traditional IRA:

A traditional IRA is an IRA that is a pre-tax way to invest for your future retirement.
This is similar to a 401k, but it is completely self-funded. The key here is all contributions are pre-tax so it lowers your effective taxable income.

When you retire and take money out the money will be taxed, but we are assuming it is taxed at a much less rate because as a retiree you will be making less money. If you take money out early the government will tax you an additional 10% to take those distributions.

As of the writing of this book you can contribute up to $5,500 per year in this type of IRA.

No matter how you choose to save for your retirement, you must start now. If you are 20 or you are 55 you have to save for retirement. If you do not save for retirement you will never retire and you will have to continue to work until you die.

Although that sounds harsh, it is true. The fact is we cannot depend on social security as it will probably not survive, in its current form. You must invest in your retirement every way possible if you want to make sure you do not have to work until you die.

Invest smart and invest in your future and you will not have to work your entire life.

Chapter 9

Loans
Home equity/ Line of credit

Once we have built our credit and we have a home there are ways to make sure we have money available to us if we need it. As you pay down your principal in your home you build what is called equity. A quick example of this is as follows:

Value of home: $250,000
Mortgage left: $180,000
Home equity: $ 70,000

The equity is basically money that you would have if you sold the home. This is used to form a base of money available to you called a home equity loan. Banks will loan you money based on this amount. With this amount, your credit and the ability to pay it back. They do there calculation and tell you how much they can lend you. Remember they do not want to take your home because they are banker's not real estate people, but with this type of loan, they can and will if you default.

A home equity loan may or may not be a good idea. In my opinion there are not many reasons to take a loan like this. If you are taking a loan like this to blow it on stuff or something frivolous it is definitely not a good idea.

I know a guy who, during the run on real estate in the early 2000's took an equity loan and bought a Lamborghini. He was a customer of mine and it ended up costing him a lot more then he planned for. Now anyone that knows me knows I am a fan of exotic cars, but I know not to put my home at risk. That is a prime example of taking equity from your house for something reckless.

Do not borrow money for things you normally would not be able to afford. That is the worst thing you can do.

A good reason to take a home equity loan is to modify or improve your home. Improving your home to increase resale value can be a good thing, but remember it is an additional loan that you will be required to pay payments on. You will also pay interest on the loan which as with your mortgage can be quite a considerable amount. In the example below a home equity loan can really change your budget situation.

Example:

Mortgage:	$1,250
Taxes:	$350
Insurance:	$200
Total:	$1,800

Add in your home equity Loan
$50,000 paid in 15 years @ 4.5%

$385.00

Total would now be $2,185 per month

This is a 21% increase in your base home expense. This is before electric, water, garbage, cable, etc. If you go for a home equity loan, make sure you are willing to and able to pay the payment or not only will you default on a loan, but you will put your home in jeopardy. It is a very risky proposition and many people have lost their homes to not being able to pay their home equity loan.

Again, they can be used effectively if you need to take money to do things such as home repairs or improvements. If you can get the money another way such as a 401k loan it is better choice and you do not have to pay a bank interest. As discussed before you pay yourself back the interest in a 401k loan.

A home equity line of credit is similar as you are using the equity in your home to get a loan. This one, however, is more like a credit card as you can pay back and take more money on demand.

There are rules that go along with that, but it is more for people that need to be able to take money, pay it off, and then take money again. But again this is a risky loan as it involves your home and you are using it as collateral.

If you are going to take a home equity line of credit or loan beware that if you default you will put your home in jeopardy.

Like any loan you take out, you must be able to pay the payment on the loan or you can jeopardize your credit. The only additional thing with this loan is if you default you also put your home in jeopardy. Be very careful with these types of loans make sure you can handle the payment. Home equity loans are just a risky proposition.

Chapter 10

Medical, Home, Car and Life Insurances
The savings are in the details, choose carefully

In this chapter, I want to help you understand insurance and what insurances you need and what insurances you might not need. Health insurance is a major thing, right now, so of course we will spend some time on that and then go into some of the other insurances you have available to you.

We are going to discuss the many different insurance programs available for you to use. Insurance is usually used to avoid an extreme expense and would not be used for items or things you can afford to risk. An example would be if you buy a new car, you buy insurance just in case something happens.

The $30,000 cost of the car is well worth insuring it for $1,800 per year because if something happens you are protected from loss.

General rule would be if it costs more over x period of time don't buy the insurance. This is a risk vs. reward.

There are other insurances that are required, i.e. home insurance on a mortgaged house. Over the next few pages we will go through the most common insurances and how they work.

Again, insurance is a way to reduce your risk in hopes you do not have to use it. The insurance companies also hope you do not have to use it as they charge more if you are more of a risk. If you are less of a risk they charge less. An example of this would be a 60 year old person will pay less for car insurance then a 17 year old who just got his license. They are anticipating that the 60 year old will be more cautious and will not drive as recklessly as a 17 year old who just got his license. There are many different types of insurance from car insurance to pet insurance, you can pretty much insure anything.

Health Insurance:

So you want to get health insurance? Well now you have to get it with the new regulations that the government has imposed on us. Let's discuss health insurance first. Health insurance is available in all different forms.

The main ways you can get health insurance is from your employer or from individual purchase. Both insurances offer the same choices, but if you are lucky enough that you employer provides it you will save money being part of a group plan.

This new change to our healthcare system has some advantages, but also has a lot of disadvantages. The idea behind it was that people want healthcare and are willing to pay for it. This, unfortunately, has not worked out and the main thing it has done is drive healthcare costs up.

This is the most common insurance that people purchase and is a rather big purchase now days ranging from a low of $3,000 upwards of $15,000 for full family plans. Now that the "healthcare penalty' is taken out of the tax code at least it is not mandated.

That being said there are a few types and parts of the current health system. On the following pages are the different pieces that make up available health insurance. As of this writing there are new laws and the healthcare system may once again change.

PPO:

The first and most popular type of healthcare plan is the PPO plan. The PPO is short for "participating provider organization"
These plans are a group of doctors, facilities and hospitals that have agreed to give reduced rate healthcare to members of the insurance carrier. They negotiate all charges and fees beforehand.

As long as your doctor or healthcare facility has an agreement with your insurance company your insurance will be accepted. You can choose any doctor that takes PPO plans.

HMO:

The HMO or health maintenance organization is a plan similar to the PPO as being a health insurance to get all medical care. The difference is that with an HMO you chose a primary care physician who acts as the "gatekeeper" for all your medical needs. You have to go through the primary doctor for any referrals other than emergency care. This is a cheaper option, but it is sometimes difficult to manage.

Within the different plans there are all variables in your deductibles that range from very high to low.

Getting and maintaining insurance is a personal choice and should be based off your medical history and how much you use the doctor. Most plans have copay for doctors' visits so you know you have a fixed cost for every visit vs not having insurance and paying whatever the actual visit costs.

One great benefit that was created was a way to pay all these copays and prescription costs through payroll deductions. You might have the opportunity to take part in what is called an FSA.

FSA:

An FSA is a health savings account. How this works is every time you get paid they take money out that goes toward your medical costs or potential medical costs. You normally get a credit card to utilize when you have prescriptions or medical related expenses such as copays or deductibles.

The maximum amount that you can put into an FSA as I am writing this book is $2500.00 per year. You must use this money, in the current year, or you do lose it.

HSA:

An HSA is similar to the FSA in that it is pre-tax. The difference is an HSA can carry from year to year and your employer will usually also contribute to it on your behalf. This is included in some higher deductible health plans.

Dependent Care FSA:

The next great program that you can take advantage of is a Dependent care FSA.

This is used exclusively for dependents so if you have 10 kids running around or even just one you definitely need to utilize this for your child care needs. When you pay for your daycare you can use this to pay for your daycare "pretax". This means you are saving money on your taxes while paying your daycare costs. The total, as I write this book that you can save in a DHSA is $5,000.00 and again you must use the money if you put it in the account so you do not want to put more in it than you use. You can use this for any child care or even elderly care if you have a parent or grandparent that is a dependent of yours.

With the current state of healthcare it's a constantly changing situation and this is just written to give you an idea of what is going on and how to navigate through the current state of health insurances. Please read all details of any insurance plan that you are considering.

The last health related insurance I want to discuss in this chapter is Disability insurance. There are two different types of disability insurance and most employers that offer insurance for their employees offer both types. The first one is Short term disability insurance or STD. I know, I know, who wants to get STD!?! Kind of a funny name, but it's a very serious and important insurance to have.

STD:

This can be used for any sickness that keeps you out of work more than 14 days. This kicks in to keep you up to date with your living expenses if you have a serious illness that requires you being out of work for an extended period of time.

One example of this is a pregnancy that the woman is put on bed rest.

This would be something that would qualify for short term disability and the insurance would kick in after 14 days.

This is an insurance that is very cheap and can pay major dividends, if you need it, and cost you a fortune if you don't have it. I know a few people that wished they had it when they got into a similar situation.

So you start collecting on short term disability insurance, but it only lasts for a short time hence the name "short term". If you run through your STD you will hope you have LTD or long term disability. This is another optional insurance that most companies do offer.

LTD:

Long Term Disability insurance is a very reasonably priced insurance that is very useful if you ever get seriously ill or injured and cannot work for a long period of time.

I talk to many new employees every year and these are two insurances that I always recommend to everyone because it is similar to Life insurance in that if you don't have it your family will be left out in the cold.

Without STD and LTD if you get hurt or seriously sick you can leave yourself, as well as your family, in a very poor position, without your income. STD and LTD both pay up to 60% of your salary, up to a certain amount and most even offer upgrades up to 80% of your salary. This by far is one of the most important insurances you can opt into.

Moving on past your own health we are going to talk about a few different insurances that you can take advantage of. Some of them are required by law and some of them are optional coverages that are meant to reduce your liability.

Car insurance:

Car insurance is one of the required insurances, but there are different types of car insurances. The main insurance that is required just to drive a car is Liability insurance.

You must have liability insurance if you are going to drive a car, but this only covers injury and repair to a person or car that you hit, it does not cover your vehicle. In "no fault " states you are also required to have PIP coverage which basically covers you and any of your passenger's in case of an accident.

This type of insurance is good if you have a very old car that is paid off. An example of this would be if you had a car that was worth $2,500 and the Full coverage insurance would cost you $1,500 per year. It probably wouldn't be smart, in that case, to get full coverage insurance.

As I mentioned, in the example above, the next type of car insurance is Full coverage insurance. This includes collision and comprehensive coverage. This covers you and anyone that you are in an accident with. It also covers fire, theft, flood, and glass coverage.

There are many different deductibles and coverage amounts to choose from so not to complicate things I will not go through the different deductibles and coverage limits. I will give you an example of what coverage looks like. Below is an example of a coverage amount that you could choose. The example is also the minimum coverage that you need if you lease a car.

Example:

100/300/50 coverage:
100 means $ 100,000 bodily injury liability per person
300 means $300,000 bodily injury per accident
50 means $50,000 personal property per accident

Like I said before there are many different deductibles and coverage amounts offered by insurance companies so see your insurance broker for more details.

Home insurance:

Homeowners insurance is required by the bank for any home that still has a mortgage on it. This has to be factored into any home purchase that you make. Generally, home insurance covers for replacement of the structure due to fire or storm. In areas where hurricanes occur, this cost is the majority of your insurance fee.

In addition to the fire and storm protection it normally also covers theft and vandalism for both the outside and contents of the home. You must get the proper coverage that matches the value of the home. If you do not get the proper coverage you can be under insured and if something happens it will not cover the full cost of replacement of your contents and structure.

The insurance also normally covers liability so that if someone gets hurt on your property you are also covered. There is typically a deductible for normal theft and fire coverage at a set amount but when dealing with storm coverage there is normally a percentage of the total amount insured.

Keep in mind, homeowners coverage is normally for free standing homes as condos and town houses normally fall under the homeowners association and the only thing it does not cover is contents and interior walls. In these cases, you should get coverage through Renters/condo insurance. We discuss those in the next section.

In short, it is not only required, but it is a needed thing to have homeowners insurance no matter if you have a mortgage on your home or you own it outright. You need to have homeowners insurance to protect yourself.

Renters/Condo Insurance:

Renters insurance, as I mentioned in the previous section, is for the contents of a rented apartment or owned condo/ townhouse. The whole idea of having this insurance is when you purchase a condo/townhouse the HOA normally covers the outside insurance for fire/wind/ and storm, but they do not cover anything inside such as your property and the interior walls of the home.

Theoretically, if you do not have this insurance and a fire burns down the building everything will be covered by the insurance except the inside of your home.

The building will be rebuilt, but you will never be able to reoccupy your home until you pay to repair the unit. This insurance is a must if you have a condo/townhome. Now the original design of this insurance is to protect renter's personal property. If you are renting and the place burns down you don't have to worry about rebuilding the unit, but you do have to worry about your contents.

If you are renting an apartment or house or you own a condo/townhome you really need to look into renters/condo insurance to protect not only from fire/ wind/ storm you also need to make sure you are protected from robbery. It's really a good thing and it is reasonable compared to the cost if all of your possessions are stolen or destroyed.

Life insurance:

The final insurance that I want to discuss is Life insurance. Life insurance is not for you, it's for the people you leave behind when you die. Life insurance is not a fun thing to purchase as it's something you will never personally use, but in the event that you die before you are old and prepared, it will help your family to pay bills and be able to continue to live the lifestyle they are used to. I put this in the book as an FYI and do not pretend to be an expert in life insurances. For this book I will give you the basics.

There are two types life insurance that you can purchase, one is Term life and the other is Whole life.

Term life insurance is a more affordable type of life insurance. It offers coverage for a specific amount of years for a specific monthly fee. This is usually renewable yearly for x amount of years and the premium generally goes up as your age goes up.

Whole life is insurance is a more expensive form of life insurance. This insurance has a set payment and as long as it's paid, it will not go up. This type of insurance also has a cash value if you ever need to discontinue these policies you can cash them in as there is a cash value.

You can insure virtually anything. It's up to you what you choose to do and as you accumulate wealth you need insurances less. Use insurance wisely and you can protect yourself from undo stress by making sure you are protected.

My general rule of insurance is to insure anything you cannot incur the full cost of if it is destroyed, lost or stolen. Some insurance just does not make sense as the cost over time outweighs the cost of the item.

Always weigh all your options before you purchase any type of insurance. If you fear something is too costly not to protect, get the insurance. It will give you piece of mind. Just make sure it fits in your budget.

Chapter 11

Debt Management strategies

You went to school, you buy a car, you have fun, now you have the debt, and how are you going to pay for it??

Debt is something that we obviously do not want to get into. In this book I'm trying to make sure you never get into a financial situation that you cannot get out of.

Some will say debt is good, but I can tell you the less debt you have the better off you will be. If you have debt and you are paying interest you are wasting money that you can be using for other things.

Let's look at a quick example of how you can get into credit card debt and how you should get out of it.

Example of typical credit card debt:

CARD	TOTAL OWED	% OF INTREST	MIN PAYMENT	PROMO APR
1	$1,000	20	$30	NO
2	$1,000	5	$35	NO
3	$3,000	0	$100	YES
TOTAL	$5,000		$165	

As you can see this is pretty much standard as far as the average person in the United States. Once you are at this point it is easy to continue to pay the minimum payment and keep charging more on the card. This is what the credit card companies want you to do. They want you to keep paying minimum payments and paying the interest every month. Card number 1 will turn into over $2000 and you will be paying for 20 years, if only the minimum is paid.

There are many options on this, but my favorite way to pay these off is to pay off the highest interest cards first. My opinion in this specific case is to pay the highest interest one off first and once that one is paid move on to the next highest interest card. This will limit your total interest paid on credit cards. This method can be applied to any loan you have. The key is to make sure one, you pay your bills on time and two you make sure you limit the interest you pay on these loans/ credit cards.

I advise you that once you get to a point that your payments are not manageable you must stop using the credit cards. The easiest way to do this is put the cards away and do not carry them with you.

As I mention in the earlier chapters you should always take advantage of zero interest credit cards which help you leverage your money while getting what you need now. You do need to make sure that you can afford to pay these off before they go into the interest period or you will be charged interest from the inception of the loan.

It is very important to budget yourself using the budgeting tools that I have included in this book. Sticking to a budget and not over extending yourself with credit card debt is a key to your financial future. Being very careful what you purchase is the key to building up your wealth.

You will hopefully have a very long life and you will have plenty of time to buy all the cool stuff you want.

The key to managing your debt is budgeting and self-control. This is easier said than done. If you are committed to making sure you do not work all your life just to live pay check to paycheck you can do it.

This takes discipline, but in the end, it will be worth it because you will be able to retire and live well.

Chapter 12

Wealth building
Why be rich when you can be wealthy?

When people say they want to be rich they really don't know what they are talking about. What is rich anyway? Is rich being able to do what you want whenever you want? Does it mean you don't have to work or be able to have whatever you want? Really there is no definition, it is a personal thing. The question is; what is rich to you?

In this chapter, I give you a little info on wealth building. What is wealth building you ask? My definition is making your money work for you. We can make a whole book on investing so I am just going to give you some basics and my opinion on how to handle them.

First, we are going to talk about stocks. There are many ways of investing your money and trying to make it grow. One of the best ways is in the stock market.

I do want to warn you that this is also one of the most risky ways to grow your money. Your principal is not protected and you can potentially lose your entire investment. While this might seem scary to some there are ways to limit your risk when dealing with the stock market.

I included this chapter in the book to give a brief overview and in no way want you to be under the impression that this chapter will teach you how to make money in the stock market. I simply wanted to give a brief overview.

I recommend that people start their investment with a very little amount of money to learn how the system works. There are many different sites online that you can choose from. I recommend Scottrade/TD for its ease of use and $7.00 buy or sell trades.

We are not going to discuss options in this chapter so for our purposes there is two ways to make money off the stocks. The stock goes up and you sell it or the stock pays dividends. Dividends vary from stock to stock, but can be from $0.1 per share and up. I have had stocks with annual dividends equal to $3.00 per share. Most are in the .05-.25 range.

You deposit the money into the account and then you are welcomed to the exciting world of stock trading. The first thing you want to learn are the terms and what they mean as related to stocks.

The online trading programs offer the opportunity to buy stock at a set price and also sell at a set price. This is a very useful tool because with this you can program a buy order to purchase stock at a certain price.

Let's get right into some terms you need to know.

Market order:

This is an order to buy or sell stock at the current stock trading price.

Limit Sell order:

This is an order to buy or sell stock at a specific price. Example: A buy order set for $25.00 will only buy the stock when it goes down to $25.00. In this case, you will be expected to buy the stock for the maximum of $25.00. Once the price hits $25.00, it becomes a market order.
At the same time if you set a Limit Sell order the stock will only sell when the price is $25.00 or higher. It gets triggered when the stock hits $25.00 and becomes a market order.

Stop order:

This is a sell order to stop loss. It is generally used when you are making profit on a stock, but expect it can go down.
An example of this would be a stock you bought for $20.00 and the stock goes up to $24.00.

You were expecting to make 10% and you are now up 20% and you want to retain 15% with the option of making more. You set a stop order for $23.00. Now if it goes down to $23.00 it will trigger a sell order. If it goes up, it will do nothing and you can watch your profits go up.

Stop- limit order:

A stop-limit order is an order placed that combines the features of a Stop order with those of a limit order. A stop-limit order will be executed at a specified price, or better, after a given stop price has been reached. Once the stop price is reached, the stop-limit order becomes a limit order to buy or sell at the limit price or better.

The following real example demonstrates this:

Ctsx is trading at $74.52 and you want to buy this stock "on sale" so you put in a buy order for "$72.00. You program the buy order on 7/15/20xx. The order is triggered on 7/25/20xx and you buy the stock for $72.00. By the end of the trading day it is back to $73.20. If you were to sell at this point you made $1.20 per share.

The smart thing to do here is as soon as the purchase is made set a sell order. If you look for say a 5% rate of return on each trade you would set the sell order as a limit sell order for $75.10. If that stock goes up to $75.10 the sell order will be triggered and the stock will sell for at least $75.10.

You can also use a stop order to sell a stock if it goes below a certain amount.

Let's say the same stock has gone up to $74.99 and you want to make sure your profit is protected you can set a "stop" order to sell if it goes below 74.89. This order will be triggered if the stock price goes down to $74.89. This type of order could sell for less as once it is triggered it becomes a market order. So if it is not a sharp decline it could sell for anywhere under that stop price of 74.89.

In this specific example you made money, but I do not recommend starting with a high priced stock such as this example. I would start with Stocks under $20 if you are going to start your investments with less than $5000.

This will allow you to buy more of a particular stock.   With a $15.00 stock you can buy 200 shares at $3000. So for every $1.00 that stock goes up you make $200.00.   If you see that stock has a 52 week range of say $13-$23 you might be in a great situation to make some serious money.

Research, research, research. Study and watch the stock before you buy it. Know all your fundamentals and do not make impulse decisions. You will make mistakes and you will have loses along with the gains, no one always wins so be prepared for that and make your trades with that in mind.

There is plenty of information online if you would like to get well versed in trading. Please make sure you do your research before you start investing.

Chapter 13

Putting it all together to WIN!!!

I hope that so far you have gained a lot of useful information you can use in the real world to manage your financial life. In this chapter I want to summarize how to put this all together to win in your financial life.

5 Simple rules:

1. Do not spend more than you make (This seems obvious but many people do not follow the first rule.)

2. Limit your costs on depreciating assets. (A car is a depreciating asset, purchasing a new one every three years will cost you a fortune over your life time.)

3. Avoid interest payments at all costs.

4. If you use credit cards. Pay balance every month. (If you are already in cc debts then pay at least 20% more than the minimum payment every month)

5. Save at least 10% of you gross household income. (This can and should include a 401k plan or IRA)

Change of mentality:

As I stated before, if you are in school, just graduated or are 50 years old, in order to become successful you have to fundamentally change your mentality.

This isn't a corny think positive book; it is an opinion on how to build wealth by watching what you do with your money. It is not too late to change the way you see your future. That said you cannot achieve any of the plans in this book with a negative attitude. You might be asking yourself now, "how am I supposed to be positive when I'm in debt to everyone"?

I will tell you it will not be easy, but you will determine if you can save and build wealth. No matter what you do for a living, if you budget accordingly, you can build your lifestyle that you will enjoy. Is it hard to follow these rules? Yes you have to become disciplined in how you spend and look at money. Get all negative phrases out of your head and do not let them come out of your mouth. If you are negative a lot of times it's for a reason, you have been raised with that negativity or been in an environment that it thrives.

If you are in that situation I can tell you that people from my experience do not want you to succeed. They will tell you things like, you can't or it won't work!

Get away from those people that are negative. They will bring you down.

One of my favorite or should I say least favorite ones is "the rich get richer"! That is an excuse statement, dare I say a loser mentality. Let's think about what someone that says that statement is saying; they are saying no matter what you do you will always have less money and opportunity then someone that has the money now.

Completely untrue, some of the world's wealthiest people started with nothing, but a positive attitude and an idea that they were going to be successful.

You must go into this planning and knowing that no matter how much money you make you can make your money work for you and live a very comfortable life. What you do now will affect your next 10 years. Plan out your future the way you want it to look. If you want to retire at 55, use this book to make a plan to do it. Don't wait, do it now.

Bonus Chapter

Making more out of your job

The whole point of this book is to teach you how to manage your money to enable you to retire young enough and wealthy enough to enjoy yourself. Working in management in corporate America I have seen thousands of different personalities and attitudes that go with them. You might be asking yourself as you read this chapter, "why is he preaching about good career habits in a financial freedom book"? The reason is that no matter what you do someone has to pay you in order to use good behaviors in managing your money.

Without your own business or working for someone you will have no money to manage. That being said there are different traits that I found make someone successful.

These are very important in everything you do.

1. Attitude
2. Willingness to complete projects
3. Timing
4. Vision
5. Demeanor

I worked my way up in a fortune 500 company from the bottom at very young age. I do not think I am smarter than the average bear; I just have the attitude and will to get any job done.

Through the years I thankfully had the support of my family to guide me through the ins and outs of working for a company and making the most of every opportunity.

The reason some people are successful and some people are not (whether employed or self-employed) boils down to the 5 things at the beginning of this chapter. We will go over all 5 and my opinions on them in this chapter.

As I said before I am not saying I'm smarter than the average bear or that my opinions are gospel, but this is the way I see it and hopefully my advice serves you well.

1. Attitude:

Whether they were raised with the attitude or became disgruntled at some point. The common denominator I have seen in unsuccessful people is poor or negative attitude. On the other side of this coin are successful people having the reverse, they have a positive attitude. I'm saying you can have a great attitude and money will fall from the sky, NO! But I can promise a lot more opportunity if you have a can do attitude.

The first thing a manager or boss picks up on is your attitude and if you portray everything she/he asks you to do as a problem. They will pick up on this and label you as the problem.

Let me give you an example. Your employer gives you a task to do that you really dislike. You can do three things, not do it and quit, be upset and do it anyway, or accept the fact that she/he pays you to work and do the job the best you can. Now the first one will have you looking for a new job, the second one will get the task done, but ruin your day and possibly some of the company's customer's days.

The third option will get the job done, you'll get paid and your employer and customer will be happy. As a matter of fact if it's a particularly tedious task you will most likely be held in high regard by your employer for getting it done with a great attitude.

The third one is the best choice, but it is also a choice that requires rational thought and a positive can do attitude.

Ask yourself, what would you do in the above situation? If you answered 1 or 2, you know you need to check your attitude. If it was the second one, most likely your manager, if they are any good will pick up on the negativity and remember it.

There are people out there that are not smarter then you and have no more or less ability that will do the job you have with a smile on their face and that is what your manager is looking for.

Up until a few years ago I did not think you could train or teach attitude adjusting, but since then I have proven that it works.
The only caveat to training for a good attitude is the participant has to be willing to change. This requires you to not only believe that your job and you are important, but it requires you to respect the job you are currently doing as the best job for you at this time.
Attitude is up to you and only you can make that choice.

2. Willingness to complete projects and be on time:

The second thing that can make or break your career is how you do your job. When you complete a task it should be complete and on time.
It sounds simple, but in a work environment if you consistently strive to be thorough, you will stand out from the rest of the work force. Remember in school if you did not turn in an assignment on time it was a zero, so how does it happen in the work world?

In the bosses' mind or in your customer's mind if you are self-employed every zero adds up and at the end of the day you will either be fired or you will lose your customers. In the work force we get graded on what we deliverer.
Nothing should be missing, no mistakes, double and triple checked. No matter what the job is your boss should not have to come to you and say you completed this and x and y were not done.

Careless mistakes should not happen and if you check your work several times, they will not. If something is due Monday your manager/customer should have it Monday complete and ready for the next step.

Making sure a project is complete even at the most trivial level shows your employer or customer you really care about what you do. This leads to further opportunity and more money to save!
The reverse is true if something is late or not complete.

Your manager or customer will think you do not care and you will not be looked at for promotion or additional business. This includes any small mistake including grammar, punctuation, and sentence structure in emails. You must be precise in everything you do.

3. Timing:

   Timing is a funny thing that is often looked at and confused with luck. Timing is not luck it's the insight that time is correct now to do something. If you have a great attitude and you have the willingness to complete projects, on time, your timing will fall into place. Let me give your simple example. You're going to cross a street; you see cars coming so you see that the car is going slow enough that you can cross. You move and cross the street. Was that luck? No, it was timing! The same is true in your career. Timing is basically logic based hope that something will work in your favor.
   In business it is not as easy as crossing the street, but the same principles work. If you work harder than the next person, in your same position, you will get noticed and you will move up. The person that works the hardest and makes sure he/she is open to any work will get the bosses' or customer's attention.

4. Vision:

   Your vision for yourself is one of the most important things. If you do not know where you want to go you cannot expect you will get there.

To clarify, you need to have a vision or plan for what and where your life is going to end up.

As I stated previously in this book you must have a plan. This can include everything from your work to your personal goals. You must not only have these goals, but vocalize them so you are expected to achieve them. Make sure you have a vision of what and where you want to be, both financially as well as personally.

5. Demeanor:

Your demeanor is how people see you and how you interact with others. You can be the smartest person in the room, but have a poor demeanor.

When this is the case, you will not be recognized and you will not advance in your career or anything you do. On the other hand, if you have a great demeanor you will attract attention and set yourself up to have many opportunities in your professional and personal life.

These five things I have discussed will insure you success in whatever you do as a career. Although it is easier said than done this is something you should work at and will surely make you more successful in your life.

Thank you for purchasing my book and I hope you have learned ways to manage your financial life. I wrote this book to try to help as many people as possible to have a very strong financial life and make sure they are not a prisoner to their debt.

The key is to take this step by step and do not overwhelm yourself with trying to do a 180 degree turn in your financial life. This is a process that you must strategically work on throughout your life. Your finances will change, your status will change and you must be able to adapt and change with the times. My hope is this will help you navigate through the financial aspect of your life not only today but through the years.

I wish you the best in your financial life.

Greg Saladino
YMMBook.com

Made in the USA
Monee, IL
08 March 2022

92479201R00075